mad about science

Objects & Materials

JOHN CLARK

ReD KiTE

Welcome to Mad About Science: Objects & Materials!

All the objects in the Universe, from shooting stars to bouncing balls, are made of matter. Materials are the many different kinds of matter. Read on to discover the weird ways matter behaves – the pages are packed with colourful illustrations, useful information and incredible facts. Science has never been so much fun!

Throughout the book, there are fascinating experiments that are fun and easy to do. You'll find most of the things you need for them in your home. You can get other items, such as insulated wire and bulbs in bulb holders, from shops that sell electrical supplies. Look up your nearest one in your local phone book. Follow the instructions for each experiment carefully and always take care with sharp tools and electrical equipment.

If you want to find a particular subject, just look it up in the index at the back. Otherwise, simply turn to page 4 and let the fun begin!

Contents

First published in the UK in 2001 by Red Kite,

an imprint of Haldane Mason Ltd, 59 Chepstow Road, London W2 5BP. email: haldane.mason@dial.pipex.com

Copyright © Haldane Mason Ltd, 2001

ISBN: 1-902463-42-0

A HALDANE MASON BOOK

Editor: Ambreen Husain **Designer:** Rachel Clark **Illustrators:** Phil Ford and Peter Bull Studios **Educational Consultant:** John Stringer BSc

Colour reproduction by CK Litho Ltd, UK Printed in the UAE

Picture Acknowledgements

Balfour Beatty 20; **Bruce Coleman Collection** /Mark Taylor 7, /Jeff Foott 11, /Johnny Johnson 12, /Dr Eckart Pott 25, /Kim Taylor 26; **Eye Ubiquitous** /Bennett Dean 18; **Sydney Francis** 14; **Image Bank** 4; **Oxford Scientific Films** /London Scientific Films 9, /Colin Monteath/Hedgehog House 12, /David Cayless 21, 23, /Robert Winslow 29; **Re-Cycle** 30; **Science Photo Library** /Oscar Burriel 17.

Note: The experiments described in this book are designed to be safe and easy to carry out at home. The author and publishers can accept no responsibility for any accidents that occur as a result of using the book. If in doubt, consult an adult.

The Material World

Everything around you that you can see or touch is made of matter. So are some of the things you can't see, such as the air. In fact, all the objects in the Universe, from an exploding star to the hairs on your head, are made of matter. So 'matter' is really just another word for 'stuff'! There are three main kinds of matter: solids, such as rock; liquids, such as water; and gases, such as air. This book is all about matter and the weird ways it behaves.

Kites are made from paper or plastic because they are light, flexible materials.

4

Make the most of matter

There is an amazing array of materials – different kinds of matter – around us. Some are natural, such as wood and cotton, and some are artificial, such as plastic and fibreglass. Others are a combination of two or more materials. To make them easier to deal with, scientists sort them into groups depending on their physical and chemical properties. But what does that mean?

Physical properties include things like strength, heaviness and bendiness. For example, can the material be stretched or bent, or does it break? Does it conduct (carry) electricity or heat well? How much weight can it hold? How heavy is it for its size? And how hot does it have to be before it melts?

Chemical properties are to do with what happens to materials when they are burned or mixed together. For example, does a material catch fire easily? Does it dissolve in water? Does it mix with other materials? Is it safe to eat, or a poison?

So what's the point of all this? Well, once we understand a material, we can work out how to use it. That's why bridges are made of steel instead of sticky tape, and why we use washing-up liquid instead of wallpaper paste to clean our dishes. The more we know about materials, the easier it is to come up with new inventions to improve our lives.

Try this!

Sort it out

Collect together various things made from different materials – a stone, a paper clip, a stainless steel teaspoon, a coin, a plastic bag, a piece of cooking foil, an eraser, or whatever else you can find. Now arrange them into various groups. For example, put all the things that are hard in one group, and all the things that are soft into another. Or sort them into things that are easy to squash when you squeeze them and those that aren't. You could also split them into a group of things that seem heavy for their size and those that seem light. Use a magnet to test which things are magnetic and which are not. How many other ways of sorting them can you think of?

Amazing fact

The bones inside your body are stronger for their size and weight than steel – and so is a single hair from your head.

Did you know?

Nearly a third of the materials that make up a modern car are plastics. They are also used to make TV sets, trainers, computers, clothing, bowls, bags – the list seems endless! Plastics are fantastic because they can easily be moulded into the shapes we want. The first plastic materials came from nature. They included rubber, made from the sap of a tropical tree, and cellulose, the main substance in wood pulp and plant fibres. Today, most plastics come from the chemistry lab. There are now dozens of plastics, and their names often begin with 'poly–', such as polythene. Can you think of any more?

You use many different plastics every day.

Rock Solid

When we want to describe how firm and strong something is we often say it's 'as solid as a rock'. Other solid materials include bricks, concrete, wood, metals and most plastics. All solids have some things in common. If they are small enough we can get hold of them and pick them up. They are usually rigid and keep their shape. But what is it about solids that makes them like this?

Inside a solid

Everything – solid, liquid or gas – is made up of tiny particles called atoms. They are so tiny that you can only see them through a very powerful microscope. It would take several million of them side by side to make the thickness of the paper you are looking at. Atoms can be joined together in combinations called molecules.

The atoms or molecules inside a solid are packed closely together. They can hardly move from their positions, and this is why a solid keeps its shape. In many solids, the atoms or molecules always have the same regular arrangement – these are called crystals (more crystal facts on pages 18–19).

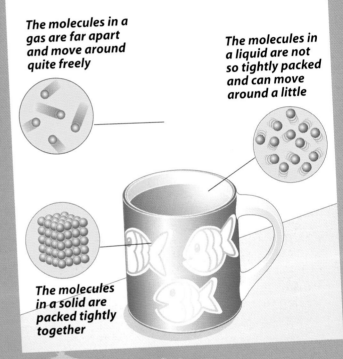

The molecules in a gas are far apart and move around quite freely

The molecules in a liquid are not so tightly packed and can move around a little

The molecules in a solid are packed tightly together

Mighty metals

Metals are one of the most important kinds of solid. They are strong and can be formed into different shapes. If you leave a metal spoon standing in a hot drink, the spoon handle soon gets hot as well. This is because metals are good conductors (carriers) of heat. That's why metals are used to make saucepans. The wires that carry electricity around your house are made of copper, another metal, because metals are also good conductors of electricity.

Amazing fact

Rubber is elastic because of the shape of its molecules, which take the form of long zig-zag chains. When you stretch rubber, you pull the chains straight. But when you let go, the molecules snap back to their original shape.

6

Try this!

Current conductors

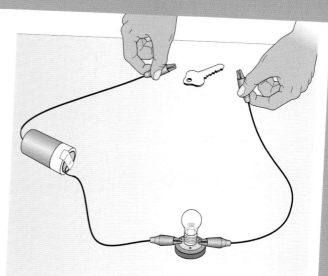

You can test whether a material is a conductor of electricity by including it in a simple circuit using a battery and a bulb in a bulb holder. You'll also need three lengths of insulated wire, four crocodile clips and sticky tape. Tape the bare ends of one wire to one end of the battery, and attach a clip to the other end. Clip it to the bulb holder. Tape the second wire to the other end of the battery and put a clip on its end. Put clips on both ends of the third wire and clip one end of it to the bulb holder. Make sure the circuit works by touching the clips together – the bulb should light up. Now try completing the circuit with various materials, such as metals, carbon (sharpen a soft pencil at both ends to test the 'lead') and non-metals. If the material conducts electricity, it will complete the circuit and the bulb will light.

Try this!

Heat test

Get a metal spoon and a plastic spoon of the same size. Use a dab of butter to stick a frozen pea or a small sweet near the end of each spoon handle. Put the spoons into a mug that is half full of hot water and watch what happens. The pea on the metal spoon slips off first. Why? Because the metal spoon is better at conducting heat up its handle to melt the butter. Plastic, on the other hand, is a bad heat conductor.

7

Did you know?

There is one way to disturb the regular arrangement of particles in a solid – heat it. Ice is a very common solid, especially in winter. It is solid water. In ice, the water molecules are held in a regular structure. When you heat ice, the heat energy makes the molecules move about, out of their crystal positions. As a result, the ice melts and becomes a liquid – which we know as water!

As ice on branches or buildings slowly melts, it moves downwards, forming icicles.

Flowing Liquids

Unlike a solid, a liquid, such as water, has no fixed shape. It just takes up the shape of whatever you put it in! This is because the atoms or molecules that make up a liquid are farther apart than in a solid and, although they are still attracted to each other, they are free to move around more. Liquid can splatter against a wall, break up into drops and join together again, and be poured, stirred or spilled.

What's liquid like?

Although the molecules in a liquid can move around, they resist being squeezed closer together. So if you apply pressure at one place in a liquid, it is transmitted equally through all of it. You can see this effect when you squeeze toothpaste out of a tube. Even if you squeeze at the very end of the tube, the paste still comes out at the other end. In the same way, a liquid can transmit a force. That's why liquids are used inside hydraulic machinery, such as car brakes. The braking system is made up of pipes filled with liquid – brake fluid – and pistons that apply pressure to the liquid.

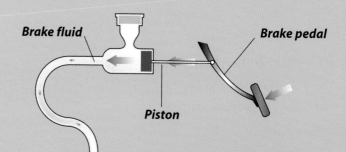

Brake fluid   Brake pedal

Piston

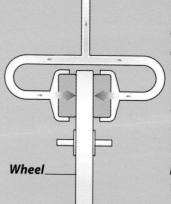

Wheel

When the driver presses on the brake pedal, a piston tries to squeeze a liquid in the brake pipes. The force is transmitted along the liquid in the pipes to the wheels, where it presses other pistons to apply the brakes.

8

Amazing fact

Glass looks like a solid, but in fact it's a liquid! It's so viscous that it moves very, very slowly – so slowly you can't see it. Very old windows have a wobbly surface from the glass flowing down the pane, while new windows have a flat surface.

Go with the flow

Some liquids are much thicker than others. A thick or sticky liquid, such as shampoo or runny honey, is said to be viscous. Oil is an important viscous liquid. Its viscosity makes it a good lubricant because it tends to cling to the moving parts of machinery and reduce friction between the parts. A thinner liquid, such as water, would flow away.

The surface of a pool of water is like a stretchy skin, so pond skaters can walk across the water without sinking.

On the surface

Have you ever watched insects walking on the surface of a pond? Water boatmen and pond skaters are two insects that can do this. But why don't they sink? The surface of the water seems to have a stretchy 'skin' on which the insects walk. This effect is called surface tension, and it happens because molecules of water cling together at the surface.

Try this!
Surface science

To see surface tension in action, you'll need a needle and a small square of tissue paper slightly larger than the needle. Fill a bowl nearly to the top with water. Place the needle on the tissue and carefully lay them on the surface of the water. Soon the paper soaks through and sinks, leaving the needle 'floating' on the surface, held up by surface tension. What happens if you make a few waves with your fingers?

Did you know?

Surface tension is what makes soap bubbles round. The tensions on the inside and outside surfaces of the thin film of liquid that forms the bubble pull it into the smallest shape possible, which is a sphere.

9

Try this!
Thick and thin

You can compare the viscosity (thickness) of liquids – as long as they're transparent! Try it with water, cooking oil and a really thick liquid such as golden syrup (ask whoever bought the syrup first). Take three jars or glasses and fill each of them with one of the liquids. Drop a marble into the water, and use a watch with a second hand to time how long it takes to fall to the bottom. Then do the same with the other liquids. Which takes the longest?

What a Gas!

Most gases are hard to find! You can't see them, smell them or touch them – but they do exist. Air, which is made up of lots of gases, surrounds us all the time. There are also many other gases, such as the helium which fills fairground balloons, and the natural gas we use for heating and cooking. Like a liquid, a gas has no fixed shape. But unlike a liquid, it will not stay in its container unless you put a tight lid on it!

Gas facts

The atoms or molecules that make up a gas are far apart. They zoom around constantly, bouncing off each other and off the walls of whatever container they happen to be in. As a result, the gas completely fills the container and pushes against it. This pressure can be put to good use. For example, the pressure of air inside car tyres gives you a smooth ride. Compressed air also powers those pneumatic drills you see (and hear) being used to break up roads.

The air we breathe is a mixture of gases. Only one-fifth of it is oxygen, which we need to breathe. About four-fifths of it is a gas called nitrogen. There are also traces of other gases, such as argon, neon, carbon dioxide and water vapour (the gas form of water).

10

Eagles use thermals to hover high above the ground while they scan the area below for prey.

A lot of hot air

When air is heated it expands – the warmer molecules move around more and spread out more. This makes the air lighter, so it begins to rise. Watching ashes of burnt paper rising above a fire inspired the French Montgolfier brothers to construct the very first hot-air balloon in 1783. On a large scale, air heated over warm ground rises in columns called thermals. Glider pilots and soaring birds such as eagles use thermals to carry them upwards.

Thermals also play a big part in the weather. Warm air near the ground can hold invisible water vapour. But as it rises high in the sky, the air gets colder. The colder air can't hold as much water vapour, so some of the vapour condenses – it turns into droplets of water that form clouds. If it gets even colder, the water droplets join together to form even larger droplets, and it rains.

Did you know?

English chemist Joseph Priestly (1733–1804) discovered oxygen in 1775. During his many experiments with gases, he dissolved carbon dioxide gas under pressure in water – the result was fizzy water. His discovery began a European craze for soda water!

Fizzy drinks and 'sparkling' spring water have carbon dioxide in them – they are carbonated drinks. Next time you enjoy one, think of Joseph Priestly!

Did you know?

Two important gases, hydrogen and helium, are less dense, and therefore lighter, than air. Because of their low density, both gases have been used for filling airships. But hydrogen catches fire easily, which caused several disastrous airship crashes in the 1930s. Modern airships are filled with helium, which does not burn.

Amazing fact

The gases argon, krypton and neon occur in air in such small quantities that they are called the rare gases. When electricity is passed through traces of these gases sealed inside a glass tube, the tube glows with bright colours. Neon produces a bright red light. Neon lights are often used in shop and street signs.

11

Try this! Hot-air balloon

You will need an adult to help you with this. Take a large paper (not plastic) bag, 20–25cm square, and hold it with the mouth of the bag open and downward – make sure there are no holes in it. Now blow warm air from a hairdryer (on its low setting) into the bag. The warm air is less dense (and therefore lighter) than the cooler air outside the bag, so the bag should float upwards when you let go of it (but make sure you turn the hairdryer off first!). This is how a hot-air balloon works.

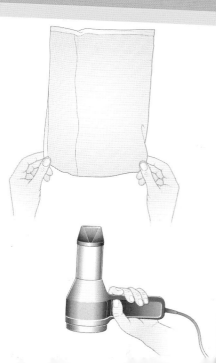

All Change

Whether a material is a solid, liquid or gas depends on how its molecules move. This in turn depends on how hot or how cold it is. Heat a cold solid and its molecules move farther apart until it melts. Heat the liquid and its molecules move even farther apart until it forms a gas. These three forms – solid, liquid and gas – are known as the states of matter. Scientists call the change from one into another a 'change of state'.

State to state

The temperature at which a heated solid changes into a liquid is its melting point. The temperature at which a heated liquid changes into a gas or vapour is its boiling point. These changes of state are physical changes, and they can be reversed. Cool a gas enough and it changes into a liquid. Keep on cooling the liquid and it eventually turns back into a solid. The temperature at which a cooled liquid changes into a solid is its freezing point.

The change of a gas into a liquid on cooling is known as condensation. You can observe condensation by breathing on a mirror. The water vapour in your breath condenses to tiny water droplets that form a misty film on the glass. A few solids, such as iodine and solid carbon dioxide (dry ice), are unusual because they can change directly from a solid into a gas. This is called sublimation.

When a candle burns, some of the wax melts in the heat of the flame. The hot liquid wax drips down the sides. As it cools, it becomes solid again.

12

Did you know?

Deep below the ground, temperatures are much higher than they are at the surface. This means that the rock there sometimes melts! When it gets even hotter, and pressure builds up, boiling hot, liquid rock is squeezed out of cracks in the Earth's surface, making a volcano. Once it reaches the air, molten rock – called lava – soon cools and turns back into solid rock.

Amazing fact

Mercury – the liquid in some thermometers and barometers – is a liquid metal! Most metals only melt into liquid when they are incredibly hot. Mercury is the only metal that is liquid at normal room temperature.

A matter of size

Because a rise in temperature makes molecules move farther apart, most solids expand (get bigger) as they get hotter. That is why engineers leave spaces in bridges and railway lines – to allow for expansion in hot weather. Otherwise they would buckle as they increased in length. It works the other way too – most solids get smaller as they get cooler. But ice is different – it gets bigger as it cools. That's why ice in frozen water pipes can expand even more and burst the pipes if it gets even colder. It also means ice is less dense, and therefore lighter, than water. That's why icebergs and ice cubes float. Icebergs in the Antarctic can be larger than the tallest buildings and up to 100km long, but they still float!

Try this! Ice pressure

Completely fill a plastic bottle with water (do not use a glass bottle) and screw the cap on tight. Place the bottle of water in a plastic bag and put it in the freezer. Leave it for a day and then take it out. You'll probably find that the water expanded as it froze, bursting the bottle.

This iceberg is even larger than it looks because about 90% of an iceberg floats beneath the surface.

13

Did you know?

If water seeps underground and meets very hot rocks, it heats up, boils and blasts out of the surface as a column of steam and water, called a geyser. Any water in its way is also forced upwards as a hot spring. Scientists are now working to use this heat – called geothermal energy – as a source of clean power for the future.

There are several geysers in Yellowstone National Park, USA. They blast out columns of steam and boiling water every hour or so.

Watery World

Water is one of the most important types of matter in the world. Nearly two-thirds of the Earth's surface is covered with it. Most of it is in the seas and oceans, but there is also water in lakes and rivers, and frozen into snow and ice around the Arctic and Antarctic ice caps. However, most water does not stay in one place. It moves around the Earth in the water cycle.

The never-ending water cycle is vital for life on Earth.

Round and round

The energy that powers the water cycle comes from the Sun. The heat of the Sun warms the water in lakes, rivers and oceans, which hold 97% of the world's water (the remaining 3% is frozen in the ice caps). The heated water evaporates, changing into water vapour that rises in the air. The vapour may form tiny water droplets, which are moved around by the wind.

Water vapour forms clouds

Water evaporates

Water vapour condenses, falling as rain, sleet or snow

Higher in the atmosphere, water droplets gather together to form clouds. If the wind blows clouds off the sea and over land, or if clouds have to rise to get over mountains, they get cooler. This makes the vapour condense, and tiny droplets merge together to form larger drops. When these drops become too heavy to stay in the clouds, they fall as rain. If it's very cold, the raindrops may freeze and fall as hail, sleet or snow.

Most of the rain falls in the oceans, where it starts the cycle over again. But some rain falls on the land. It flows into streams and rivers, which eventually flow back to the sea. In this way, water is constantly changing state, driven by the energy of the Sun.

Did you know?

The ice in hail and snow is a type of solid crystal. Snow crystals have six-sided or six-pointed shapes, and every single one is different. Snowflakes form when the crystals join together as they fall, melt and then freeze again. But they will reach the ground as snow only if the air temperature is freezing all the way down.

Snow crystals are made of frozen water vapour.

Did you know?

Nearly all the ice in glaciers and the polar ice caps originally fell as snow. It was slowly squashed into ice under its own weight. Some parts of the Antarctic ice cap are more than 4km thick. If it melted, the sea would rise by more than 70m.

Amazing fact

As hailstones tumble around inside a cold cloud, they grow bigger and bigger as more and more ice crystallizes on to them. They can be as big as tennis balls and weigh up to 1kg. They've been known to break windows and dent cars!

15

Try this! Making clouds

Here's how to make a mini-cloud inside a bottle. Fill a plastic bottle with hot water from the tap (don't use boiling water). Let it stand for a few minutes and then pour away all but a quarter of the water. Now stand an ice cube on the open top of the bottle and watch your cloud form! The ice at the top cools water vapour inside the bottle, so that it condenses into tiny water droplets – just like a real cloud.

Disappearing Act

A spoonful of sugar contains thousands of small crystals – as you'll notice if you spill them and have to clear them up! But stir the hard sugar crystals into a glass of water, and they disappear! At least they seem to. If you taste the water, you can tell the sugar is still there – so why can't you see it?

Simple solutions

Like most solid substances, sugar crystals are made up of millions of molecules. When you put them in water, the molecules can break free of each other. They are too small to see, but they are still there, floating around among the water molecules. This is called dissolving – the sugar has dissolved to form a solution. The thing that dissolves – in this case, sugar – is called the solute, and the liquid it dissolves in is called the solvent. Water is a solvent for many substances – which means there are lots of things that dissolve in water.

Not all substances are soluble (will dissolve) in water, and that's a good thing, too. How else could we drink water out of glasses, or sail boats in the water? Chalk, wax and wood are all examples of substances that are insoluble (will not dissolve). Can you think of others?

Many tablets are made to dissolve in water – it makes them easier to take and our bodies absorb them quicker

There is a limit to how much sugar – or any other substance – you can dissolve in a given amount of water. But, you can usually dissolve more of a substance if the water is hot. If you dissolve sugar in hot water, then let it cool, crystals will begin to appear again – because cold water can't hold as much as hot water can.

16

Try this!

Find the limit

Put some warm water into a jug or large jar and add spoonfuls of salt, stirring in between. Count the number of spoons until no more will dissolve. You have made what is called a saturated solution. Repeat the experiment using the same amount of water at the same temperature, but dissolving sugar instead of salt. Which is the more soluble, salt or sugar? What happens if you use cold water?

Try this! Separating colours

A solvent (the liquid part of a solution) can be used to separate mixtures. A simple way to see this is by using ink, which is a mixture of different pigments (coloured substances). You will need a glass, some blotting paper, a black felt-tip pen and sticky tape. First, put about 4cm of water in the glass. Next, cut a strip about 4cm wide from the blotting paper – its length needs to be about 2cm shorter than the height of the glass. Make a big spot near one end using the felt-tip pen. Use sticky tape to attach the other end of the strip to the middle of the pencil. Balance the pencil across the top of the glass so that the strip is dipping into the water, but make sure the spot is not in the water. As the water seeps up the paper it will carry the pigments from the ink with it. Some move farther than others, and so the different

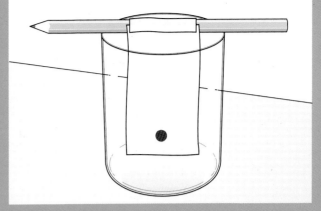

pigments separate. Scientists often use this method, called chromatography, to separate mixtures. Try this with other colours and see what happens!

Amazing fact

About 50g of solid material leaves your body every day dissolved in your urine. Some of this material, mostly calcium, can separate out of the solution in one of your kidneys and form a large stone. The largest kidney stones can weigh more than 1kg.

17

Jelly is a type of gel. It comes in different colours and flavours.

Did you know?

Dissolving is just one of the ways one substance can be 'dispersed' in (completely mixed in with) another. Here are some more:
▶▶ A gel (like the jelly you eat or hair gel) is a special combination of a liquid and a solid.
▶▶ Foam (like shaving foam or fire-extinguisher foam) is a gas dispersed in a liquid.
▶▶ An aerosol (like hairspray or spray paint) is a liquid dispersed in a gas.
▶▶ Smoke is a solid dispersed in a gas.

Crystal Tips

A crystal has a regular structure of atoms or molecules. Most solids, apart from living things (and things that were once alive, like wood and cotton), are made up of crystals. Crystals have geometric shapes, but you can't always see the shapes because the crystals are too small. Some crystals have such beautiful shapes and colours that we wear them as jewellery.

Crystal clear

A perfect crystal has straight edges and flat, smooth 'faces' or sides. Some crystals sparkle because their faces reflect the light when you move them around. Crystals that are valued for their beauty and rarity include gemstones such as diamonds, emeralds and rubies.

The shape of a crystal depends on the arrangement of the atoms that make it up. For example, the atoms in salt are arranged in cube patterns, so salt crystals also take the shape of cubes. There are only six basic crystal shapes, and any one substance always has the same crystal shape. So all salt crystals, no matter where they come from, are cubes.

To become a perfect crystal, a solid has to form freely with space around it, so that it doesn't get squashed. In nature, one of the main ways this can happen is when a molten substance cools and turns into a solid. Metals consist of crystals made in this way, and many

In hot countries with coastlines, such as India, people have salt farms. They collect the salt crystals that form as sea water in shallow pools evaporates under the heat of the sun.

18

kinds of rock contain crystals that grew as the molten rock slowly cooled and solidified. Some of these mineral crystals are as big as a car.

Crystals can also form when a solution evaporates. For example, when a salt solution – salt dissolved in water – evaporates, the water turns into water vapour and floats away in the air, and the salt molecules join together into regular crystal shapes. This often happens at the edges of seas and salty lakes in hot countries.

Try this!

Dish of crystals

Make a strong solution of salt by stirring several spoonfuls of it into a cup or jar of hot water. Put some of the salt solution in a saucer and leave it somewhere warm for a few days, such as on a window ledge in the sunshine. The water will evaporate away and the dissolved salt will reappear as a deposit of crystals.

Amazing fact

The numbers on digital watches and pocket calculators are made of patterns of liquid crystals held between two pieces of glass. Electricity is used to change the patterns of the crystals so that they form numbers. This is called an LCD, or liquid crystal display.

Did you know?

Crystals can be used in jewellery, but they also have other uses. Diamond is the hardest substance in the world, so it is used to make drills for drilling down through rock to reach deposits of oil. Rotating discs used for cutting stone and concrete are also coated with industrial diamonds. Quartz crystals can be made to vibrate in a perfectly regular time sequence, so they are used in quartz clocks and watches. Silicon crystals are in the silicon chips that make computers work.

19

Try this!
Growing crystals

Make a strong sugar solution by adding as much sugar as will dissolve in a mug or jar of hot water. Next, take a short length of thick thread or thin string and tie one end to the middle of a pencil. Balance the pencil across the top of the jar so that the thread hangs into the solution, then leave your experiment alone for a few days. After a while, sugar crystals will appear at the end of the thread. The longer you leave the thread hanging, the bigger the crystals will grow.

Mix and Match

Salt and water are easy to mix together – you just stir the salt in and it dissolves. But not all substances mix this easily. What about two solids, such as salt and sand? You can put them together, but neither one dissolves and you can separate them again afterwards. Two liquids may mix perfectly, like vinegar and water, but other pairs of liquids can be very hard to mix.

In the mix

Solids, liquids and gases can all be mixed together – some more easily than others – to make new materials. Cement is made from clay, chalk and water that is mixed together and put through a special process. This requires special equipment and takes quite a long time. But simply mix cement with sand, gravel and water, leave it for a while, and you have concrete – a very useful material!

You would think all liquids would mix – and many do, such as water and juice or tea and milk. But what happens if you try to mix oil and water? The oil just sits on top of the water. If you shake them together very hard (ideally in a bottle or jar with a lid!) they will mix for a little while. But leave the bottle to stand, and the oil and water will gradually separate again.

Although oil and water don't like mixing, you can make them mix – and stay mixed – by mixing in a third substance called an emulsifier. This kind of mixture is called an emulsion – tiny blobs of a liquid dispersed in another liquid. Mayonnaise is an emulsion. Other common emulsions include cosmetics such as face cream. This is made from an oil such as liquid paraffin or lanolin, which is combined with water, using soap as the emulsifier.

20

Concrete is used for the foundations of buildings and bridges, as well as on roads and pavements, because of its strength.

Amazing fact

Some substances react so violently when they mix that they are used as rocket fuel. The thrusters that steer the Space Shuttle in orbit use fuel made from two chemicals that burst into flames as soon as they mix.

Try this! Clever colouring

Put equal volumes of cooking oil and water into a large glass jar. They will not mix but will form two layers, with the oil on top. Now carefully add a few drops of food colouring. It will sit as globules on the top because it does not mix with oil. Use a spoon to stir the whole mixture. The food colouring will immediately mix with the water and colour it. What happens to the oil?

Try this! Separating solids

How do you separate salt and sand? One way requires a magnifying glass, a pair of tweezers, a steady hand and lots of patience. It would take a long time. There's an easier way with a little help from science. Here's how it works. First make a sand and salt mixture by stirring together equal quantities of both in a jar of water until all the salt dissolves. Now pour the mixture through a coffee filter paper, or a sieve lined with a strong tissue. The sand stays on the paper, because sand doesn't dissolve in water (if it did, beaches wouldn't last long!). Next, you can recover the salt from the water by letting the remaining solution evaporate (heating it helps). The salt crystallizes out as the water evaporates.

21

Did you know?

The same stuff you use to do the washing-up can clear up an oil slick! Detergents, such as washing-up liquid, break up grease so that water can wash it away – so they are great for washing clothes and dishes. They can also break up larger amounts of oil, such as oil spills at sea which can otherwise kill wildlife and damage beaches.

If oil spills at sea are not broken up, the oil can wash up on to beaches.

All About Soil

Soil is one of the world's most important mixtures. It's a combination of water, gases, bits of rocks and minerals, and the remains of dead plants and animals. Nearly all plants, from small grasses to giant forest trees, need soil to grow in – and all animals ultimately depend on plants for food. So we all owe our lives to soil!

In the mix

Soil is a mixture of different materials, so how do they get mixed together? Rainwater helps, and so do plant roots and burrowing animals such as worms. But soil still has different layers. The dead plant and animal remains, called humus, are found in the uppermost layer of soil, while stones and fragments of rock are mostly found in the bottom layers. And soil in different parts of the world, or even within one garden, contains different mixtures of ingredients – that's why some plants thrive better in one place than in another.

In fact, scientists have identified thousands of different soil types! Sandy soils let water drain through them easily, while others (called clay soils) are sticky and heavy so water doesn't drain through quickly. Some soils, such as peaty soil, are dark in colour and contain lots of humus. Peaty soil is often found on boggy ground. Chalky soil, on the other hand, is pale and stony, with only a small amount of humus, and water drains through it very quickly.

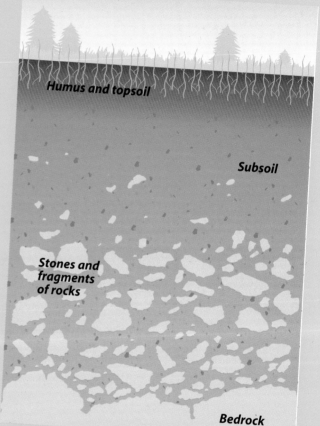

Humus and topsoil

Subsoil

Stones and fragments of rocks

Bedrock

Soil science

Scientists study soil by separating it into its different parts. One way of doing this is to break up the soil as much as possible and then sieve it into smaller and smaller particles. Another method is to stir a sample of the soil into water and then leave it to separate into layers. The biggest, heaviest bits fall to the bottom first, and the smallest bits end up on top.

22

Try this!

Soil study

Collect two or three small samples of soil from different places – such as your garden, a plant pot, and a park.

To find the soil type, wet a small sample and rub it in the palm of your hand to see if it is smooth (clay-rich soil), gritty (sand-rich soil) or full of lumpy, dark-coloured humus (peaty soil).

To test the drainage, put a sample of soil in a funnel. Hold the funnel over a jar and pour in some water. How quickly does the water pass through?

To check the particle sizes, shake each soil sample through a kitchen sieve. How much passes through the sieve and how much is left behind?

To check the composition, add each soil sample to a jar of water, screw on the lid and shake well. Then leave the samples to settle. You should see the different layers,

with the densest layer (sand and stones) at the bottom and the lightest (clay) on top. Humus will float on the surface of the water.

23

Did you know?

As well as worms, spiders and insects, soil is full of even smaller, tiny living creatures. They are not pests – they improve soil by digesting dead plants and animals and breaking them down into rich, fertile humus. Their burrowing also improves the texture of soil by letting air into it. However, a few soil animals do harm plants by eating their roots or spreading diseases.

Worms do a great job of mixing up soil and rotting plants in compost.

Chemical Reactions

If you dissolve salt in water, you can get it back by letting the water evaporate. And if you mix sugar and sawdust, you can – if you have several hours to spare – pick out the sugar again. But what happens if you set fire to a mixture of sugar and sawdust? After the smoke and flames die down there would be nothing you could do to get the sugar and the sawdust back. That's because they have been part of chemical reaction.

When you mix together and bake the ingredients for a cake , the heat changes them into a new – and very tasty – substance!

24

Changed forever

In a chemical reaction, two or more substances combine to make something entirely different. And it's usually impossible to reverse the process. Millions of chemical reactions are taking place every second around us and even inside us. All the processes that keep our bodies growing and moving are made possible by chemical reactions.

Other everyday chemical reactions take place in cooking, inside batteries in things like torches and toys, and in fireworks and explosives. None of these reactions can be undone. For example, you can't 'uncook' a cake and change it back into eggs, butter, sugar and flour.

Burning question

There are many different types of chemical reaction. One of the most common is oxidation – when a substance combines with oxygen. And one of the most common types of oxidation is burning. Burning something – like sugar, sawdust, petrol or rocket fuel – is called combustion. In this reaction, the substance, or fuel, reacts with oxygen in the air to give off energy – as well as other substances. For example, when a fuel such as petrol, oil or candle wax burns, it gives off heat and light energy, plus water and a gas called carbon dioxide. Because humans burn so much fuel, we now have a problem with too much carbon dioxide, which some scientists think builds up around the Earth and causes global warming.

Try this! Inflating fizz

You will need a small, plastic fizzy drinks bottle, a funnel, some bicarbonate of soda, some vinegar and a balloon. Pour a little vinegar into the bottle. Use the funnel to pour a spoonful of the bicarbonate of soda into the balloon. Then carefully stretch the neck of the balloon over the neck of the bottle and lift up the balloon so that the bicarbonate falls into the vinegar. The vinegar reacts with the bicarbonate to produce carbon dioxide gas, which then begins to inflate the balloon.

Did you know?

A chemical reaction called photosynthesis happens inside plant leaves. The plant combines water from the soil and carbon dioxide from the air using energy from the Sun. They react to produce food that keeps the plant alive and helps it to grow.

25

Did you know?

In a chemical reaction, things that react together are called reactants. The things that are created are called products. Reactants and products can be completely different from each other. For example, when sodium – a soft, silvery metal – reacts with chlorine – a poisonous, choking green gas – they turn into pure white sodium chloride crystals – otherwise known as everyday salt.

Amazing fact

A hectare of corn – that's about the size of one and a half football pitches – produces enough oxygen by photosynthesis every day for 325 people to breathe.

Oxidation Options

Burning is just one type of oxidation – a reaction between a substance and the oxygen in the air. Oxidation can happen quite slowly (think of a barbecue or a log fire that can burn for hours) or very fast, as in a big explosion that gives off lots of heat and light. It can also happen very slowly indeed – for example, rusting is another kind of oxidation.

26

Many different substances containing metals produce the colourful display when a firework explodes.

Reaction force

The simplest oxidation reaction happens when hydrogen burns in oxygen. The only product (apart from heat and light energy) is water. That's why space rockets, which run on hydrogen, are shrouded in clouds of steam at lift-off. It is also why engineers are trying to make cars that run on hydrogen instead of petrol. Hydrogen cars would produce no carbon dioxide or other pollution.

In a big explosion, oxidation happens even faster. The force of the explosion comes from huge quantities of hot gases produced in the reaction. The shock wave from the explosion causes the bang.

Rusting is an example of very slow oxidation. When iron and steel go rusty, it's because the metal combines with oxygen in the air, making a new chemical called iron oxide – or rust. There is no heat or light, but over several years rusting can destroy a car just as completely as a fast, hot fire.

Did you know?

Gunpowder is the oldest known explosive, and is believed to have been discovered accidentally by Chinese scientists in the 7th century. They may have discovered it while they were experimenting with fireworks, which they invented!

Try this! Candle magic

Stand a short, thick candle in the middle of a large glass bowl – a large mixing bowl will do – and carefully pour 2–3cm of water into the bowl. Ask an adult to light the candle and cover it with a large glass jar. Watch what happens. As the candle burns, it uses up the oxygen in the air inside the jar. The water prevents any more air getting into the jar. When all the oxygen is used up the candle goes out. Without oxygen, the combustion reaction cannot continue.

Try this! Burning is forever

Take a piece of paper and see what it feels like. Pull it along its length to see how strong it is. Then, with the help of an adult, put the paper on the ground outside and burn it completely. What does it look like now? Can it be turned back into paper?

Amazing fact

The planet Mars is known as the Red Planet because it is covered by soil that is red. And that's because the soil is rich in iron oxide – rust!

27

Did you know?

When iron reacts with oxygen, it makes iron oxide – rust. But there are forms of iron oxide that can be decorative rather than destructive. Potters can put a glaze containing iron on their pots. When the pots are baked in a kiln containing lots of oxygen, the iron is oxidized to a form of iron oxide which is red. If the kiln contains only a little oxygen, the iron oxide formed is black.

Potters can vary the amount of oxygen in their kilns to produce different shades of red and black.

Acid Test

Lemon juice and vinegar taste sour and sharp. They're acids. Bicarbonate of soda tastes bitter and has a soapy feel – it's an alkali. Acids and alkalis are substances that occur in nature, and are used in food and in all kinds of products, from wrinkle cream to toilet cleaner. But although they are useful, strong acids and alkalis can also be very dangerous.

Surrounded!

Acids are all around us. Bees, ants and stinging nettles all have methanoic acid in their stings. Tartaric acid is found in grapes and other fruits, citric acid is found in lemons, and carbonic acid is found in soda water and other fizzy drinks.

Strong acids such as sulphuric acid (used in car batteries) are dangerous – they can burn your skin and clothing. But there is a strong acid that occurs naturally in your stomach – hydrochloric acid – and it doesn't eat away at your insides. It helps to digest food. You can feel it stinging your mouth and nose when you've been sick! Nitric acid is used to make fertilizers and explosives. All of these acids are strong enough to dissolve metals.

Weak alkalis include bicarbonate of soda and washing soda. They are used in baking powder and indigestion tablets. Strong alkalis such as sodium hydroxide (caustic soda) can cause

Bee stings contain an acid. That's what makes your skin swell up if you're unlucky enough to get stung.

nasty burns if they get on your skin. They are used in oven cleaners, for cleaning drains and for making soap. Wasp stings, unlike bee stings, contain an alkali.

28

Neutralize!

When an acid is mixed with an alkali, the two neutralize each other and react together to produce salt and water. For example, hydrochloric acid reacts with sodium hydroxide to form sodium chloride, or common salt. This is why putting bicarbonate of soda (a weak alkali) on a bee sting, or vinegar (a weak acid) on a wasp sting, helps to stop the pain.

Try this!
Make your own indicator

An indicator is a substance that can change colour to show if something is an acid or an alkali. With the help of an adult, chop up a red cabbage and boil it in some water (if possible, use distilled water which you can get from a garage or motor spares shop). Throw away the cabbage, allow the purple liquid to cool and filter it through a paper coffee filter or a sieve lined with a tissue. Next, get several clean jars or glasses and put some of your cabbage juice indicator in each one. Now try dropping in substances such as lemon juice, orange juice, bicarbonate of soda, sour milk, vinegar, and powder detergent. Acids will make the indicator turn red, while alkalis will make it turn greenish-blue.

Amazing fact

Vinegar is a weak solution of a type of acid called ethanoic or acetic acid. It's used for making pickles (like pickled onions) because the acid kills the bacteria that would otherwise make the food go bad.

29

Did you know?

Acid rain – rain with a weak acid in it – can kill trees and eat away at buildings and statues. It's made when coal and oil are burned in power stations. Gases from power station chimneys react with droplets of water in clouds to form sulphuric acid and nitric acid. This can be carried in clouds for many kilometres before it falls as rain.

This statue has been damaged by acid rain.

Trash or Treasure?

In every minute of every day, someone somewhere is using a material. All materials either occur naturally or are made by combining or changing natural materials. The paper used for the pages of this book was made from wood which came from trees. The plastic for plastic bags is made using oil that is found underground. But the world's supply of raw materials will not last for ever.

Think twice

Making a bridge, a car or even a paperclip uses steel, and think of all the aluminium used to make cans for soft drinks. Everytime someone scraps a car or throws away a drinks can, the metal has gone forever – and more rubbish is produced. The same happens when a bottle or a magazine or anything else is thrown away.

There is only one raw material that can be replaced – wood. We can grow more trees for making paper, but it takes many years for a tree to grow big enough to be used. So it makes sense to recycle or re-use as many materials as we can. Old newspapers and magazines can be used for making more paper or cardboard.

Amazing fact

America produces 250 million tonnes of rubbish every year. It could be used to produce as much energy as 100 million tonnes of coal, but most of it is buried in the ground instead.

Empty glass bottles can be cleaned and used again, or crushed and melted to make new ones. Plastics are more difficult to recycle because there are so many different kinds, and most don't rot so plastic rubbish keeps increasing. But some plastics can be recycled. And now there are new plastics that will break up and rot away.

30

In this workshop, children are being taught how to repair and look after bicycles.

Did you know?

Many old bicycles are thrown away or lie rusting in garages. Re-Cycle, a charity in the UK, ships second-hand bicycles to developing countries. In poorer countries, many children walk to school and back, up to 14km a day. Most cannot afford a bicycle. With help from volunteers, children learn how to look after a bicycle. They can then ride off on a bike that might otherwise have ended up as rubbish!

Glossary

Combustion
Burning; a chemical reaction in which a substance reacts with oxygen and produces heat and light.

Condensation
The process when a vapour or gas cools and changes into a liquid. When water vapour in the air cools, it condenses into tiny water droplets.

Conductor
Something that lets electricity or heat pass through.

Dissolve
To break down into tiny bits throughout a liquid when mixed with it.

Emulsifier
A substance used to blend together two liquids that will not otherwise mix.

Emulsion
Tiny bits of one liquid dispersed (completely mixed) in another liquid.

Evaporation
The process when a liquid or solid warms and turns into a vapour or gas. As water heats up, it evaporates into water vapour in the air.

Indicator
A substance that shows if something is an acid or an alkali by its colour.

Insulator
Something that does not let electricity or heat pass through.

Matter/material
What something is made of.

Oxidation
A chemical reaction between a substance and oxygen.

Solidification
The process when something turns into a solid, or solidifies.

Solute
A substance that dissolves in a liquid to form a solution.

Solution
A substance that is made when a solid is dissolved in a liquid.

Solvent
A substance in which a solid dissolves to form a solution.

Sublimation
The process when a solid turns into a gas without becoming a liquid first.

Surface tension
An effect that makes a liquid seem to have a 'skin'. It is caused by the molecules of the liquid clinging together at the surface.

Viscosity
How easily a substance flows. Water has a low viscosity and flows easily.

31

Index